INFUSED
STRENGTH + PURITY

Tiffany Cochran

Cover Design & Layout by Abram Goff || abramgoff.com
Editor: Andrea Alley || andreadalley.com
Research: Brandon Bourdeau, Chika Monu, and Amanda Zentz

This book is dedicated to those learning to walk and to those running home.
Welcome, the road is big enough for us all.

...may you be infused with strength and purity.
- I Thessalonians 3:13, MSG -

TABLE OF CONTENTS

ABOUT THE AUTHOR

Tiffany Cochran served as the Director of Operations and Finance with Moral Revolution for over seven years. Prior to this, she was an Area Specialist with the U.S. Department of Agriculture and served in leadership at Grace Church of Avondale in Jacksonville, FL. Tiffany loves seeing people come into their identity in Christ and courageously live out their dreams! She is passionate about discipleship, leadership, healthy relationships, and wholehearted living! Her dream is to see the Church walk in the fullness of who God says she is and nothing less. Tiffany holds an MA in Organizational Leadership and is a graduate of Bethel School of Supernatural Ministry. She resides in Redding, CA and is an active member at Bethel Church.

AUTHOR'S NOTE

A few years ago, after a week of seemingly having the same conversation over and over with people, I started recognizing one common thread.

While working for Moral Revolution, people would share with me what was going on in their lives. What they believed to be true about their sexuality, situation, and God. Without fail, my inner dialogue went something like this, "I understand how you could *feel* this way and be in this mess, but religion and far off thinking about God is not going to help you. You don't need concepts. You need Him. You need His word."

No matter your religious upbringing, family lineage, or sexual history (thin with knowledge or thick with experience) everyone is looking for truth. The unshakeable, pure, sticky kind. The kind of truth that will keep on being *truth* even after we breathe our last breath. John 8:31 says, " … and you will know the truth, and the truth will set you free."

Many years ago, I was the girl sharing my broken story. What I've come to discover is the kind of wholeness and freedom, we all long for, can only be found in Him. Psalm 51:6 says,

"Behold, You desire truth in the innermost being." There is no shortcut to your freedom. You cannot fast-forward the process. Learning about God, learning the truth of His word, and allowing it to take root in you will change the way you think. It will be the very light as you walk the road of healthy sexuality.

So, I invite you to *take your time* working through these pages. Meditate on His words. Memorize them, and speak them out loud over your life. As you do, I encourage you to practice recognizing when and how certain truths affect you. Journal, wrestle, and let Him in on what is going on inside of you. For example, if a certain passage triggers you to be angry, peaceful, sad, or frustrated, then *tell Him*. Start dialoguing with Him. This is how all relationships begin and start to work. It's when both parties show up and are participating. Lastly, ask Him to increase your faith to believe His words. Knowing and believing are two different things. Be sure to position your heart to read and receive in faith what He *has said* and *is saying* over your life.

My motivation, along with Moral Revolution, is to help you along the way. So, no matter your age, relationship status, or sexuality storyline, I'm glad you're here. My hope is that you discover truth that hitches you to freedom for the rest of your life. I'm telling you, it's possible.

Stay infused,
Tiff

"We are destroying speculations and every lofty thing raised up against the knowledge of God, and we are taking every thought captive to the obedience of Christ …"

- II Corinthians 10:5 -

The Bible is not there simply to collect memory verses.
It's there so you can become established in truth and the truth can set you free.

- Graham Cooke -

HIS WORD

I remember, several years ago, coming back to the Lord after stubborn independence turned into a long stint of rebellion. I was blessed to have accepted Christ in a church that valued the Word of God. I grew up memorizing scriptures and hearing the Word taught weekly. I was in church four times a week for years! After that, came a couple years of distance and rebellion. What followed were what I call the gray years. No one tells you about those from the pulpit.

You see, when you walk with God and are surrendered to His ways, things are pretty black and white. You are connected to Him. You can feel Him, hear Him, be led by Him, and know you are safely under His protection. Life isn't always perfect, but you know you're not in it alone.

On the flipside, when you pick up independence, like picking up a stick, you're essentially telling God, "I think I can do a better job than You're doing. I'll take it from here." What you don't realize is independence is not all it's cracked up to be. It separates you from your source of life and things can get pretty cloudy without Him. Add in the consequences of your sin – pain, shame, lack of joy and peace, etc. – and this doesn't make for a good time. You realize you're not as great as God at leading your life, and you miss the days when your truth was what He said versus what you thought. After I practiced using the independent stick, I remember telling my friend, "I can't wait till things are black and white in my life again. Living in the gray is not fun."

So, if any of the above is your storyline, I want to impart a little hope. His word is powerful and has the ability to put your body, soul, and spirit back together again. My prayer is that you tread gently through this book and that you give God's word permission to change you and heal you from the inside out. You'll never regret taking Him at His word. He promises, and so do I.

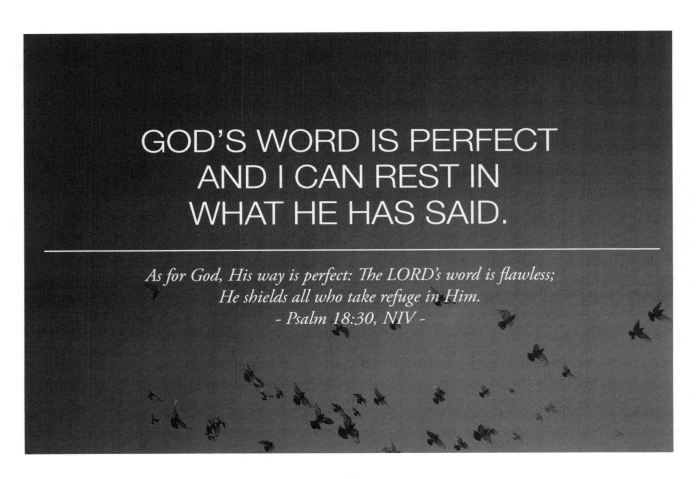

GOD'S WORD IS PERFECT
AND I CAN REST IN
WHAT HE HAS SAID.

As for God, His way is perfect: The LORD's word is flawless;
He shields all who take refuge in Him.
- Psalm 18:30, NIV -

HIS WORD IS LIKE
A GOOD MEAL TO ME!

Your words were found and I ate them, and Your words became for me a joy and the delight of my heart; For I have been called by Your name, O LORD God of hosts.
- Jeremiah 15:16, NASB -

HIS WORD STANDS
THE TEST OF TIME.

The grass withers, the flower fades, but the word of our God stands forever.
- Isaiah 40:8, NASB -

HIS WORD GIVES ME UNDERSTANDING.

From Your precepts I get understanding; therefore I hate every false way.
- Psalm 119:104, NASB -

GOD'S WORD LIGHTS MY PATH … I AM NEVER IN THE DARK!

Your word is a lamp to my feet and a light to my path.
- Psalm 119:105, NASB -

HIS WORD KEEPS ME FROM SIN.

How can a young man keep his way pure?
By keeping it according to Your word.
- Psalm 119:9, NASB -

HIS WORD SETS ME
ON A PATH OF HOLINESS.

Make them holy by your truth; teach them your word, which is truth.
- John 17:17, NLT -

HIS WORD HAS DECLARED ME CLEAN!

You are already clean because of the word I I have spoken to you.
- John 15:3, NIV -

GOD'S WORD IS POWERFUL AND HELPS SHINE A LIGHT ON WHAT IS REALLY GOING ON INSIDE OF ME.

For whatever God says to us is full of living power: it is sharper than the sharpest dagger, cutting swift and deep into our innermost thoughts and desires with all their parts, exposing us for what we really are.
- Hebrews 4:12, TLB -

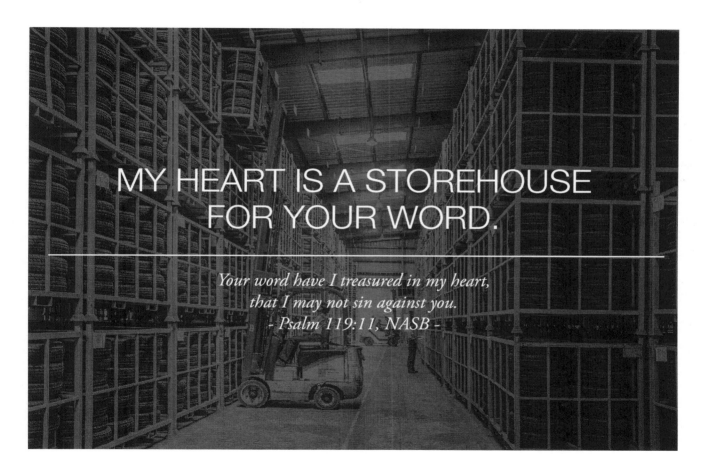

MY HEART IS A STOREHOUSE
FOR YOUR WORD.

Your word have I treasured in my heart,
that I may not sin against you.
- Psalm 119:11, NASB -

TAKE A MOMENT
TO REFLECT

———

Is there any area of your life
where things seem gray or cloudy?

———————

Is there an area of your life you don't fully *want* to trust God in?
What might the reason be? What does He say about it?

———————

What are some things you hope to see in your life
as a result of reading and meditating on His Word?

———————

Is there any area of your life you believe you don't need God in?
Have you applied an "independent stick" to that area?

Sex is good, and sex is God's.

- Kris Vallotton -

HIM

Our sexuality is one of the most sensitive and powerful areas of our life we will learn to steward. It is also one of the most private and sacred parts of our being. So sacred, in fact, that God's word tells us it is meant to be explored and expressed with only one other human being on the planet – our spouse. Wow! Our sexuality must be pretty important if God puts such a safeguard around it!

Make no mistake; this is the exact *opposite* message the world is shouting.

Living in these two conflicting messages can be challenging, especially when our curiosity beckons, our sex drive kicks in, and those awesome endorphins start flowing. Or, more common in our generation, addictions to pornography. Even more extreme, sexual innocence being violated or stolen with no one to help pick up the pieces. The bottom line is, sexuality plays a starring role in our story whether we want to admit it or not. Virgin or not, sleeping around or not, innocence lost or not … our sexuality matters and it is time to start talking to the One who created us.

Before we can have an honest conversation with God about our sex lives, it is important we have a healthy understanding of who He is. By learning His character and nature, we will feel safe coming to Him because we will know what to expect from Him.

I know talking to God about our sex drives, exploits, and frustrations can seem like a reach but think of it this way: He is the one who created you and made you a sexual being. He gets it! You're not shocking Him with your desires or questions because *He put them in you.* In fact, before Adam and Eve fell in the Garden of Eden, they walked around naked and had sex all the time - without shame! Spoiler alert: Shame was never supposed to touch your sexuality. So, make no mistake, *He* has never been ashamed or embarrassed to talk to you about sex.

Trust cannot be fast-forwarded in a relationship and this one is no different. Take as long as you need to renew your mind to who His word says He is. You'll be thankful you did when your sex drive flares up and you need to talk it out!

GOD DELIGHTS IN ME!

The Lord your God is with you, the Mighty Warrior who saves. He will take great delight in you; in his love he will no longer rebuke you, but will rejoice over you with singing.
- Zephaniah 3:17, NIV -

GOD IS FULL OF COMPASSION TOWARDS ME.

Gracious is the LORD, and righteous; Yes, our God is compassionate.

- Psalm 116:5, NASB -

GOD LOVES ME

For God so loved the world, that He gave His only begotten Son,
that whoever believes in Him shall not perish, but have eternal life.
- John 3:16, NASB -

GOD UNDERSTANDS ME;
THERE IS NOTHING
I CANNOT TALK TO HIM ABOUT!

God is almighty and yet does not despise anyone!
And he is perfect in his understanding.
- Job 36:5, TLB -

GOD IS NOT QUICK-TEMPERED.
ANGER IS NOT HIS FIRST RESPONSE.
HE DOES NOT REACT
IMPULSIVELY TOWARD ME.

The LORD is gracious and merciful;
slow to anger and great in lovingkindness.
- Psalm 145:8, NASB -

GOD IS PATIENT WITH ME.

*The Lord is not slow about His promise, as some count slowness,
but is patient toward you, not wishing for any to perish
but for all to come to repentance.*
- II Peter 3:9, NASB -

GOD IS HOLY; THERE IS NO DARKNESS IN HIM … HE IS NOT A MOODY GOD!

This is the message [of God's promised revelation] which we have heard from Him and now announce to you, that God is Light [He is holy, His message is truthful, He is perfect in righteousness], and in Him there is no darkness at all [no sin, no wickedness, no imperfection].
- I John 1:5, AMP -

GOD IS FAITHFUL. HE DOESN'T ABANDON SHIP WHEN THINGS GET HARD. HE STICKS AROUND!

God is faithful, through whom you were called into fellowship with His Son, Jesus Christ our Lord.
- I Corinthians 1:9, NASB -

GOD IS JUST, AND I CAN COUNT ON HIM TO SECURELY GUARD MY PATH. HE DOESN'T MISS A THING!

For the LORD loves justice and does not forsake His godly ones; they are preserved forever, but the descendants of the wicked will be cut off.
- Psalm 37:28, NASB -

Guarding the paths of justice, and He preserves the way of His godly ones.
- Proverbs 2:8, NASB -

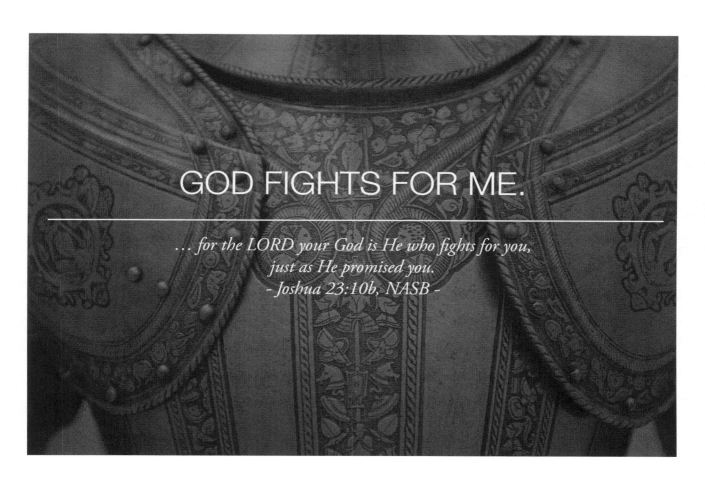

GOD FIGHTS FOR ME.

… for the LORD your God is He who fights for you,
just as He promised you.
- Joshua 23:10b, NASB -

TAKE A MOMENT
TO REFLECT

———

What truth or scripture in this chapter
surprised you the most about God?

_____

Was there any truth or scripture you had trouble believing?

_____

How comfortable are you talking to God about your sexuality?

_____

Are there any lies you believe about God that are hindering you
from talking to Him about your sexuality?

The more you reaffirm who you are in Christ,
the more your behavior will begin to reflect your true identity.
- Dr. Neil Anderson -

ME

One of the most beautiful and difficult truths I've ever had to learn from His word is what I call the *in Him* factor. I remember the day the revelation hit me about what it meant to really live, move, and have my being in Him (Acts 17:28). I had been in the church for eleven years before anyone ever explained to me what really happened at the cross and the magnitude of His resurrected life living inside of me. The hustle was over. The working for love was over. The searching for identity, value, and worth was over. I had a home, I had a name, and my place in His heart was secure forever. I felt like I was living for the first time.

Fast-forward a year and a half into my rebellious years. It's interesting to look back. I would probably tell you I overdosed on grace and jumped head first into the deep end of freedom … and He let me. That is the scary part: the free will part. He loves you enough to let you try your own thing because He knows His love is powerful enough to restore you. Your free will doesn't scare Him; it doesn't even make Him nervous. He knows that in the end, love will bring you home.

Once I came to my senses and realized I did not like doing life apart from Him, I walked home. I can completely identify with the walk of shame the prodigal son made in Luke 15. The Bible even records that he rehearsed the apology speech he would give his father. The thing is, his father ran to restore him before he even had a chance to make his speech. The son wasn't allowed to take a place among his father's servants, pay back the inheritance he wasted, or forfeit his sonship. He simply was restored.

This restoration, for me, was the longest and most painful season of my life. But it was a beautiful kind of pain. The best way I can describe it is this: His love kept breaking me and healing me all at the same time. I had ransacked His love; still He was there. I had abused His grace; still He poured it on. I had given my body away; He came rushing to restore. He would not let me go, and He would not let me "earn" my way back home. The only path He walked with me was love. There was no condemnation, not even a hint. I had never known grace like that; it ruined me and marked my life in a way I am still living out today.

So, to the many of you who have yet to discover your name in Him, this chapter is just the beginning of your journey. And to those of you who want to come home and are wondering if you can, the answer is yes, *run*, don't walk! He is waiting on the porch to welcome you home.

I AM A CHILD OF GOD.

But as many as received Him, to them He gave the right to become children of God, even to those who believe in His name.
- John 1:12, NASB -

I AM MADE IN THE IMAGE OF GOD.

*So God created man in his own image, in the image of God
he created him; male and female he created them.*
- Genesis 1:27, ESV -

I HAVE BEEN ADOPTED INTO THE FAMILY OF GOD.

He predestined us for adoption as sons through Jesus Christ, according to the purpose of his will, to the praise of his glorious grace, with which he has blessed us in the Beloved.
- Ephesians 1:5-6, ESV -

I AM A NEW CREATION IN CHRIST; ALL THINGS ABOUT ME ARE NEW!

Therefore, if anyone is in Christ, he is a new creature; the old things passed away; behold, new things have come.
- II Corinthians 5:17, NASB -

I AM CAPABLE OF GREAT THINGS!

I can do all things through Him who strengthens me.
- Philippians 4:13, NASB -

I HAVE A NEW MIND!
I HAVE GOD THOUGHTS AND IDEAS.
I PROCESS LIFE THROUGH
HIS PERSPECTIVE.

… but we have the mind of Christ.
- I Corinthians 2:16b, NASB -

I AM SEEN AS PERFECT THROUGH JESUS' EYES.

For by a single offering He has perfected for all time
those who are being sanctified.
- Hebrews 10:14, ESV -

I AM GOD'S FRIEND.

No longer do I call you slaves, for the slave does not know what his master
is doing; but I have called you friends, for all things that I have heard from
My Father I have made known to you.
- John 15:15, NASB -

I AM ACCEPTED AND COMPLETE IN CHRIST; THEREFORE, I CANNOT EARN HIS LOVE. HE LOVES ME JUST AS I AM!

Therefore, accept one another, just as Christ also accepted us to the glory of God.
- Romans 15:7, NASB -

… and in Him you have been made complete,
and He is the head over all rule and authority.
- Colossians 2:10, NASB -

I CAN NEVER BE SEPARATED FROM GOD'S LOVE; IT'S IMPOSSIBLE!

… neither height nor depth, nor anything else in all creation, will be able to separate us from the love of God that is in Christ Jesus our Lord.
- Romans 8:39, NIV -

TAKE A MOMENT
TO REFLECT

What are some things in your life that try to "name" you?
(job, position on the team, who you know, talents, etc).

———————————

Do you find it easy to look to those things for your identity
rather than what God says about you?

———————————

Do you, at your core, believe what God says about you in His word?
On your good days and bad days?

———————————

Is it easy for you to accept God's love? Or is there still a part of you that
is hustling for your identity, worth, and value apart from Him?

Religion is a very dangerous thing. By that I mean, being so caught up in rules and regulations and not focusing on the thing that matters most, a personal relationship with God.

- Joyce Meyer -

ME + HIM

Relationships can be messy. Whether it's a relationship with a friend, co-worker, or a sweetheart, they all ebb and flow differently. What may be acceptable in one relationship may not be acceptable in another. Then, factor in some other variables such as trust and vulnerability levels, seasons, and sexual chemistry and many people find themselves feeling awkward and overwhelmed. Here is where things can get a little confusing if we are not careful when it comes to our relationship with God.

First, we think God is going to treat us, speak to us, and love us conditionally the same way a human being would. False. Second, many of us weren't taught how to do healthy relationships with people, let alone God, so the lack of teaching leads to lack of trying because who wants to fail *with* God in the relationship department? (Did I hear all the perfectionists say *amen*?) Third, many of us are uncomfortable with intimacy and being known in relationships with humans. As a result, we run from a relationship with Him. We let the junk in our closets keep us from Him, and we medicate our need for companionship with friends called TV, food, porn, etc. Fourth, many of us would rather relate to God through rules (religion) versus being in an actual relationship with Him because rules feel safer. The lines seem clearer. Remember, some of us don't like messes and relationships are messy. Bonus round: if we never enter into a relationship with God then we never have to risk hearing what He has to say. This moment is a real tipping point for those with father/authority issues or those who are not ready to surrender their sin.

The problem with all of the above is none of it is true. In fact, they are all excuses rooted in fear to keep us from living in full color. So - here are a few truths from God's word that give us insight into how He promises to show up in a relationship with us. Try not to let fear or the mistakes, misunderstandings, and pain of your past/current relationships dictate your relationship with God. He is not human. He is God and how He does relationships will probably surprise and fascinate you. If it doesn't, you're doing it all wrong.

I HEAR GOD'S VOICE!

Whoever is of God hears the words of God.
- John 8:47a, NASB -

GOD HEARS ME!

But know that the LORD has set apart the godly man for Himself;
The LORD hears when I call to Him.
- Psalm 4:3, NASB -

GOD LEADS ME.

He makes me lie down in green pastures; He leads me beside quiet waters.
- Psalm 23:2, NASB -

But thanks be to God, who always leads us to triumph in Christ, and manifests through us the sweet aroma of the knowledge of Him in every place.
- II Corinthians 2:14, NASB -

GOD IS ALWAYS WITH ME!

... and surely I am with you always, to the very end of the age.
- Matthew 28:20b, NIV -

I HAVE EVERYTHING I NEED TO WALK WITH GOD!

… seeing that His divine power has granted to us everything pertaining to life
and godliness, through the true knowledge of Him who called us
by His own glory and excellence.
- II Peter 1:3, NASB -

I AM NEAR TO GOD.

---

*But now you belong to Christ Jesus, and though you once were far away from God,
now you have been brought very near to him because of what Jesus Christ
has done for you with his blood.*
- Ephesians 2:13, TLB -

MY LIFE IS MARKED BY JOY BECAUSE I LIVE CONTINUALLY IN HIS PRESENCE.

You will make known to me the path of life; in Your presence is fullness of joy; in Your right hand there are pleasures forever.
- Psalm 16:11, NASB -

GOD KNOWS ME INSIDE AND OUT!

You have searched me, Lord, and you know me. You know when I sit and when I rise; you perceive my thoughts from afar. You discern my going out and my lying down; you are familiar with all my ways. Before a word is on my tongue you, Lord, know it completely. You hem me in behind and before, and you lay your hand upon me. Such knowledge is too wonderful for me, too lofty for me to attain.
- Psalm 139:1-6, NIV -

GOD IS COMMITTED TO FINISHING
WHAT HE STARTED IN ME.
HE IS IN THIS FOR LIFE, AND HE
IS NOT AFRAID OF THE PROCESS.

For I am confident of this very thing, that He who began a good work in you will perfect it until the day of Christ Jesus.
- Philippians 1:6, NASB -

I HAVE ACCESS TO GOD …
HIS MERCY AND GRACE
ARE WAITING FOR ME!

This High Priest of ours understands our weaknesses, for he faced all of the same testings we do, yet he did not sin. So let us come boldly to the throne of our gracious God. There we will receive his mercy, and we will find grace to help us when we need it most.
- Hebrews 4:15-16, NLT -

TAKE A MOMENT
TO REFLECT

———

Do you believe God is near, or far away?

———————————

Do you believe God has value for being in a relationship with you?

———————————

Is there anything in your life you've made a "friend" that you know isn't good for you? (food, Netflix, porn, shopping, etc.)

———————————

Is there any area of your life that fear is speaking louder than God's word?

Give love away like you're made of it.

- Bob Goff -

ME + OTHERS

One glaring difference between the Old Testament and the New Testament is how straightforward and clear a priority God puts on love after Jesus' resurrection. In the Old Testament, His people were under 600 laws of do's and don'ts. Can you imagine how exhausting that would have been? Thankfully, under the new covenant, we are called to do two things: love God and others (Luke 10:25-28). He has made it so simple for us! If we can get really excellent at doing these two things, religious mindsets and works of the law will stay far from us!

So, the question now begs, what does love look like lived out in a practical way?

Our jerk reaction can often be to want to learn *how* to do relationships with the opposite sex when dating, engaged, married, or even after a breakup. To ask questions, such as: What does love look like played out appropriately in these seasons? Where is the line? When is it safe to risk? In short, we find ourselves wanting rules and concepts rather than being challenged to dig in and explore God's word. You see, "love" can get messy sometimes and when fear is center stage in our hearts it is easy to turn to rules to make us feel safe and calm our anxiety. Let's be honest, we have all been there, because sometimes rules yell louder than our heart can even whisper.

Most importantly we need to learn to do *relationships with others* well first. By doing so, we'll have tons of practice under our belt when we are finally ready to mingle and marry. Additionally, we'll be living life <u>now</u> and learn how to love <u>now</u> rather than waiting to practice "loving" once we are in a committed relationship.

So, flush your age or relationship status, God has a ton to say on what love actually look likes when led by His spirit in you. Happy practicing!

I AM AN ENCOURAGER.
MY WORDS BRING LIFE
TO THOSE AROUND ME!

Therefore encourage one another and build each other up,
just as in fact you are doing.
- I Thessalonians 5:11, NIV -

I BRING OUT THE BEST IN OTHERS!

Use your heads as you live and work among outsiders.
Don't miss a trick. Make the most of every opportunity.
Be gracious in your speech. The goal is to bring out the best in others
in a conversation, not put them down, not cut them out.
- Colossians 4:6, MSG -

I AM GENEROUS AND GRACIOUS, JUST LIKE MY DAD!

In a word, what I'm saying is, Grow up. You're kingdom subjects.
Now live like it. Live out your God-created identity. Live generously
and graciously toward others, the way God lives toward you.
- Matthew 5:48, MSG -

I KNOW HOW TO ADMIT MY MISTAKES, ASK FOR FORGIVENESS, AND RECEIVE FORGIVENESS.

Make this your common practice: Confess your sins to each other and pray for each other so that you can live together whole and healed. The prayer of a person living right with God is something powerful to be reckoned with.
- James 5:16, MSG -

I AM QUICK TO FORGIVE, I DO NOT HOLD ON TO OFFENSE AND JUDGMENT. I KNOW HOW TO LET THINGS GO.

So, chosen by God for this new life of love, dress in the wardrobe God picked out for you: compassion, kindness, humility, quiet strength, discipline. Be even-tempered, content with second place, quick to forgive an offense. Forgive as quickly and completely as the Master forgave you. And regardless of what else you put on, wear love. It's your basic, all-purpose garment. Never be without it.
- Colossians 3:12-14, MSG -

FEAR OF PUNISHMENT
DOES NOT FUEL MY RELATIONSHIP
WITH GOD OR OTHERS.

There is no fear in love [dread does not exist]. But perfect (complete, full-grown) love drives out fear, because fear involves [the expectation of divine] punishment, so the one who is afraid [of God's judgment] is not perfected in love [has not grown into a sufficient understanding of God's love].
- I John 4:18, AMP -

I AM TOUCHABLE, TEACHABLE, AND OPEN TO FEEDBACK. PEOPLE KNOW THEY HAVE PERMISSION TO SPEAK INTO MY LIFE. I WANT TO BE SHARPENED!

Iron sharpens iron, so one man sharpens another.
- Proverbs 27:17, NASB -

REJOICING, PRAYING, AND STAYING THANKFUL BENEFIT MY LIFE AND THOSE AROUND ME!

Rejoice always, pray continually, give thanks in all circumstances;
for this is God's will for you in Christ Jesus.
- 1 Thessalonians 5:16-18, NIV -

I KNOW HOW TO STAY POWERFUL, LOVING, AND DISCIPLINED IN MY RELATIONSHIPS. BY HIS SPIRIT IN ME, *I STAY ME*, NO MATTER WHAT ENVIRONMENT I AM IN.

You see, God did not give us a cowardly spirit but a powerful, loving, and disciplined spirit.
- II Timothy 1:7, VOICE -

GOD IS LOVE, THEREFORE, LOVE LOOKS LIKE THE GOD IN ME BEING EXPRESSED TOWARD OTHERS.

Love is patient, love is kind and is not jealous; love does not brag and is not arrogant, does not act unbecomingly; it does not seek its own, is not provoked, does not take into account a wrong suffered, does not rejoice in unrighteousness, but rejoices with the truth; bears all things, believes all things, hopes all things, endures all things. Love never fails …
- I Corinthians 13:4-8a, NASB -

TAKE A MOMENT
TO REFLECT

———

Are you a good steward of the relationships in your life?

———————————

Is any of your relationships in need of a tune up?

———————————

Do you love freely and without an agenda?

———————————

Is fear present in any of your relationships?

Once you've left the concept of family, you've left the concept of kingdom.

- Bill Johnson -

FAMILY

I realize this chapter may be difficult for some of you. This one word, *family*, can evoke a lot of emotions. In fact, the idea of family seems to have gotten a bad rap the past few decades for reasons, I'm sure, we can all think of.

If you look around, the definition of family seems to have undergone a "rebrand" of sorts. For example, people now identify family as their relatives, friends, co-workers, and even their local football team! This speaks volumes of the longing we all have inside of us to belong. Our desire to belong is not new to God. In fact, He understands and here is why:

Family was God's original idea because He was in one long before the world was formed. Genesis 1:26 says, "He said, 'Let Us make man in Our own image, according to Our likeness.'" Did you catch those two tiny words – Us and Our? This passage tells us that Father, Son, and Holy Spirit were all doing life together and weighed in on the creation of man and woman. If you continue reading in Genesis, man gets lonely, and God sees that he needs someone to do life with too! Thus, the creation of woman. This man and woman, Adam and Eve, go on to have children and voilà – a family is created. God completely understands and can identify with our desire to be a part of a family.

Fast-forward several thousand years and we see that the family unit has taken a beating and many have abandoned the dream of being part of a healthy and whole family, let alone, having one of their own. As you read through this chapter, let God's promises concerning family wash over you and give you hope.

SALVATION IS HERE FOR MY FAMILY!

But My righteousness will be forever,
and My salvation to all generations.
- Isaiah 51:8b, NASB -

MY FAMILY WILL SERVE THE LORD.

… but as for me and my house, we will serve the LORD.
- Joshua 24:15b, NASB -

MY FAMILY WILL TELL OF HIS GOODNESS! WE WILL HAVE A REASON TO PRAISE!

*So we Your people and the sheep of Your pasture will give thanks
to You forever; to all generations we will tell of Your praise.
- Psalm 79:13, NASB -*

MY FAMILY IS KNOWN FOR GRACE AND GENEROSITY; WE ARE A BLESSING TO THE EARTH.

*They are always generous and lend freely; their children will be a blessing.
- Psalms 37:26, NIV -*

I'VE BEEN CHOSEN TO BE A LEADER IN MY HOME.

For I have chosen him, so that he will direct his children and his household after him to keep the way of the LORD by doing what is right and just …
- Genesis 18:19a, NIV -

AS I OBEY AND HONOR MY PARENTS, GOD TAKES CARE OF ME.

Children, obey your parents in the Lord, for this is right. Honor your father and mother (which is the first commandment with a promise), so that it may be well with you, and that you may live long on the earth.
- Ephesians 6:1-3, NASB -

MY CHILDREN (PRESENT AND FUTURE) ARE A GIFT FROM GOD!

Behold, children are a gift of the LORD, the fruit of the womb is a reward.
- Psalm 127:3, NASB -

MY CHILDREN (PRESENT AND FUTURE) ARE A BLESSING TO MY LIFE!

Like arrows in the hand of a warrior, so are the children of one's youth.
How blessed is the man whose quiver is full of them ...
- Psalm 127:4-5, NASB -

MY FAMILY WILL BE KNOWN FOR JOY AND LAUGHTER! WE WILL TELL THE WORLD ALL ABOUT OUR GOD!

Then our mouth was filled with laughter and our tongue
with joyful shouting; then they said among the nations,
'The Lord has done great things for them.'
- Psalm 126:2, NASB -

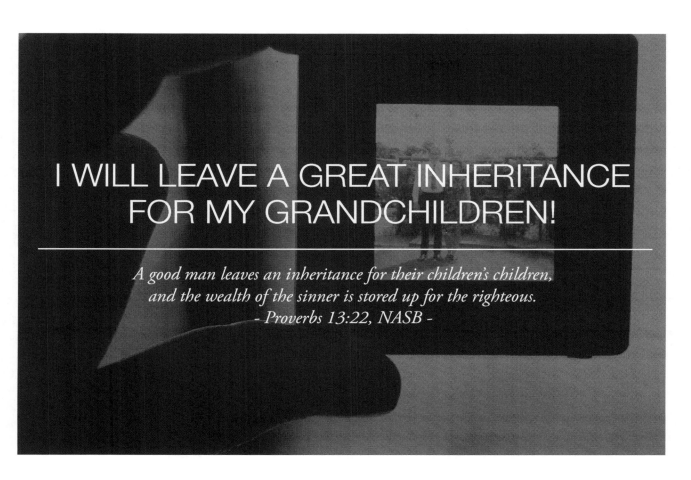

I WILL LEAVE A GREAT INHERITANCE FOR MY GRANDCHILDREN!

A good man leaves an inheritance for their children's children,
and the wealth of the sinner is stored up for the righteous.
- Proverbs 13:22, NASB -

TAKE A MOMENT
TO REFLECT

———————

What do you want your family to be known for?

_____

Is there anything in your family line that you want
to see redeemed and restored?

_____

What legacy do you want to leave
as an inheritance for the next generation?

_____

How can you begin praying for your (current or future) family today?
Get specific!

The truth is like a lion. You don't have to defend it, let it loose. It will defend itself.

- St. Augustine -

PURITY + HOLINESS

It's fascinating how much our world is obsessed with sexuality. Literally, you cannot turn on the TV without a fast food chain trying to sell you a sexy hamburger. It's pretty sad, and pretty far from the standard God calls us to in His word. There are several reasons *why* the world is trying to invite you to their sex-saturated party. Truth be told, you'd probably be pretty angry to hear them, but we will leave those for another day. If you're really curious, you can research the statistics on your own. At the end of the day, the only thing that matters is how *you* respond to the world's invitation.

Plainly put, just because the world invites you to the party doesn't mean you have to RSVP. In fact, don't even open the invite to see who will be there, what the dress code is, or what is in the swag bag. You do not owe anyone an explanation for not showing up to the party, let alone burning the invitation. You are your own man or woman and you get to decide who you are and what core values you will live by. Thankfully, God sets us up for success and gives us clear instruction in His word.

I want you to have an arsenal in heart, mind, and spirit so that when the invitation arrives – and it will – your reason for saying "no" is set and secure. Knowing His word and the value He places on purity and holiness will secure your "why" when the invitation comes and will help keep you safely away from lust (James 1:15).

My one piece of advice to you in this area of your life is *keep it simple* – trust God, obey Him, and learn to surrender your will (that part of you that thinks you know what is best for you). God knows what He is doing; He is after all, the Creator of sex! So, store up His word in your heart and don't try to go the party too early. Trust me, the morning after is not all it's cracked up to be.

GOD CALLS ME *HOLY*, THEREFORE; ALL MY CHOICES FLOW FROM MY NEW NAME!

As obedient children, do not be conformed to the former lusts which were yours in your ignorance, but like the Holy One who called you, be holy yourselves also in all your behavior; because it is written, "You shall be holy, for I am holy."
- I Peter 1:14-16, NASB -

I MAKE CHOICES
THAT BRING GLORY TO GOD …
EVEN WITH MY BODY!

So whether you eat or drink, or whatever you do,
do it all for the glory of God.
- I Corinthians 10:31, NLT -

AS I KEEP MY MIND AND HEART PURE, MY EYES ARE OPEN TO SEE GOD!

You're blessed when you get your inside world - your mind and heart - put right. Then you can see God in the outside world.
- Matthew 5:8, MSG -

A PURE LIFE IS A POWERFUL LIFE! SHAME AND REGRET WILL NOT BE THE STORY I AM TELLING WITH MY LIFE!

And let me live whole and holy, soul and body,
so I can always walk with my head held high.
- Psalm 119:80b, MSG -

GOD HAS MADE HIS HOME IN ME, THEREFORE; I WILL HOST HIM WELL.

Do you not know that your body is a house of God
where the Holy Spirit lives? God gave you His Holy Spirit.
Now you belong to God. You do not belong to yourselves.
- I Corinthians 6:19, NLV -

MY BODY BELONGS TO GOD.

God bought you with a great price.
So honor God with your body. You belong to Him.
- I Corinthians 6:20, NLV -

PURITY IS A BIG DEAL TO GOD, SO I STAY FAR AWAY FROM SEXUAL IMMORALITY!

God's will is for you to be holy, so stay away from all sexual sin.
- I Thessalonians 4:3, NLT -

I RUN AWAY FROM SEXUAL SIN!

Run from sexual sin! No other sin so clearly affects the body as this one does.
For sexual immorality is a sin against your own body.
- I Corinthians 6:18, NLT -

I AM INTENTIONAL TO STAY AWAY FROM SIN … I DON'T EVEN FLIRT WITH IT!

Keep away from everything that even looks like sin.
- I Thessalonians 5:22, NLV -

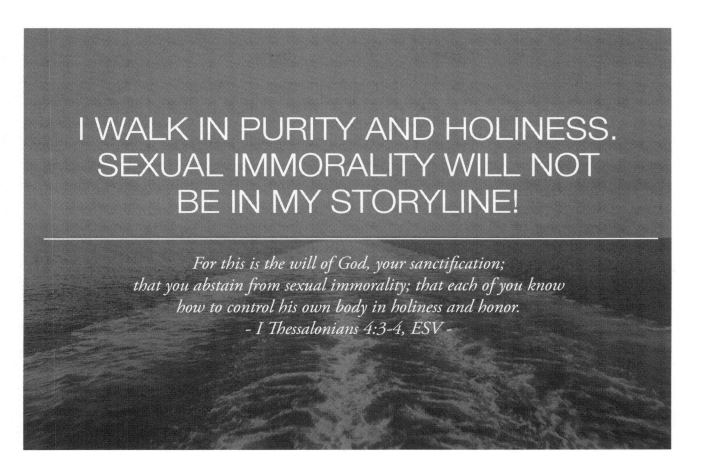

I WALK IN PURITY AND HOLINESS.
SEXUAL IMMORALITY WILL NOT
BE IN MY STORYLINE!

For this is the will of God, your sanctification;
that you abstain from sexual immorality; that each of you know
how to control his own body in holiness and honor.
- I Thessalonians 4:3-4, ESV -

TAKE A MOMENT
TO REFLECT

———————

Why do you think sex sells?

_____

Why do you think God tells us to *run* from sexual immorality?

_____

Do you believe God *really* has your best interest
at heart when it comes to your sexuality?

_____

Is your sexuality something you feel comfortable talking to God about?
Why or why not?

For what shall we do when we wake one day to find we have lost touch with our heart
and with it the very refuge where God's presence resides?

- John Eldredge -

HOPE + HEART

Hope is the output of a healthy, happy heart. Proverbs 13:12 tells us, "Hope deferred makes the heart sick, but a desire fulfilled is a tree of life." I've often heard Christians quote this scripture to me as their excuse for not having hope in their life - especially singles (wink). Many walk around thinking, "when I land the job, marry the man/woman, record the album, or (insert your dream here) then I'll be happy, hopeful, and full of joy." False.

Psalm 42:5 gives us a key to climbing out of the depths of despair and returning to Hopeville.

Why are you in despair, O my soul?
And why have you become disturbed within me?
Hope in God, for I shall again praise Him
For the help of His presence.
– Psalm 42:5

This can be a hard concept to grasp. In fact, when you read it, you might have thrown this book on the floor. But, here is the deal, it works. The key, He gives us in His word, to help us stay healthy and full of hope is His presence. *Him.* Authentic hope cannot be separated from Him; it is impossible. This should humble us and cause us to breathe a sigh of relief all at the same time. He promises that if we stay close to Him our hearts will be made well, and we will have a reason to hope. For those of us who have experimented with other tactics to give us hope, we all know they fall short and lack staying power.

I've seen so many people, myself included, try to maintain hope apart from God. It's not a fun way to live. The reality is, He has hidden hope deep in Himself and it is available to you now. He is available to you *now.* Do not believe the lie that hope is arriving on some ship when your dreams finally dock in port. God wants your heart and hope levels alive and thriving for the entire world to see *today.* In fact, your heart fully engaged with Him and dripping with hope is the enemy's worst nightmare. So, my challenge to us is this: Let's make the enemy nervous today with our heart and our hope.

I HAVE HOPE FOR MY FUTURE.

Surely there is a future, and your hope will not be cut off.
- Proverbs 23:18, ESV -

I AM OVERFLOWING WITH HOPE.

May the God of hope fill you with all joy and peace as you trust in him,
so that you may overflow with hope by the power of the Holy Spirit.
- Romans 15:13, NIV -

I MAKE CHOICES DAILY
TO CULTIVATE HOPE IN MY LIFE.

And endurance produces character, and character produces hope.
- Romans 5:4, NSV -

HOPE IS GOOD MEDICINE TO MY HEART.
HOPE KEEPS MY HEART
HEALTHY, HAPPY, AND EXPECTANT!

Hope deferred makes the heart sick, but a desire fulfilled is a tree of life.
- Proverbs 13:12, ESV -

MY HEART HAS CAPACITY BEYOND MY WILDEST DREAMS!

I pray that your hearts will be able to understand. I pray that you will know about the hope given by God's call. I pray that you will see how great the things are that He has promised to those who belong to Him.
- Ephesians 1:18, NLV -

MY HEART IS STRENGTHENED AS I WAIT ON JESUS.

Wait on the Lord; be of good courage,
and He shall strengthen your heart; wait, I say, on the Lord.
- Psalm 27:14, NKJV -

A PURE HEART IS A POWERFUL HEART; THEREFORE I KEEP MY HEART AWAY FROM EVIL.

Keep vigilant watch over your heart; that's where life starts. Don't talk out of both sides of your mouth; avoid careless banter, white lies, and gossip. Keep your eyes straight ahead; ignore all sideshow distractions. Watch your step, and the road will stretch out smooth before you. Look neither right nor left; leave evil in the dust.
- Proverbs 4:23-27, MSG -

MY HEART IS COMMITTED TO HIM!

And may your hearts be fully committed to the Lord our God, to live by his decrees and obey his commands, as at this time.
- I Kings 8:61, NIV -

I LOVE GOD WITH ALL MY HEART!

*You shall love the Lord your God with all your heart, soul, mind, and strength
… and you shall love your neighbor as yourself. 'And you must love the LORD
your God with all your heart, all your soul, all your mind, and all your strength.'
The second is equally important: 'Love your neighbor as yourself.'
No other commandment is greater than these.
- Mark 12:30-31, NLT -*

GOD'S EYES ARE ON THE HEARTS OF THOSE THAT ARE FULLY COMMITTED TO HIM! HE POINTS HIS STRENGTH RIGHT TO THEM!

For the eyes of the LORD move to and fro throughout the earth that
He may strongly support those whose heart is completely His.
- II Chronicles 16:9a, NASB -

TAKE A MOMENT
TO REFLECT

———————

How is your hope level? Heart health?
Are you thriving or merely existing?

––––––––––

Do you have a tendency to live in Hopeville everyday, or do you believe
you'll get your key to hope once your dreams are realized?

––––––––––

How different would your life look
if you began your day in His presence?

––––––––––

Do you have any areas in your life where you feel hopeless? What is the truth in God's
word you can use to combat hopelessness in these areas?

Don't you think I hear the whispers
those subtle lies, those angry pleas
they're just demons,
demons wishing they were free like me.

- *Diamonds* by Johnnyswim -

FORGIVENESS

Sin is a tricky thing, especially if we are talking about the sin of lust. James 1:15 says, "Then when lust has conceived, it gives birth to sin; and when sin is accomplished, it brings forth death." Whoa, death? That feels like an enormous consequence to lusting, and yet, there it is plainly written in black and white.

Many people have had a hard time taking God at His word on this one particular passage. However, I can tell you from personal experience, He knows what He is talking about. He wasn't lying.

You see, it's one thing to sin and realize it was sin after the fact. It's an entirely different deal when we know something is sin (our motivation and negotiation skills aside) and choose to do it anyway. It gets dangerous because it gives us the illusion that we are independent, and it hardens our hearts and dulls our spirits. Sin also can make us feel isolated and far from God and then – BAM – we're in a cycle of hopelessness, shame, and regret. No thank you.

If this is your storyline, you are going to need to know and put to memory what His word says about forgiveness. Learning how to receive forgiveness and walk it out daily, after you have gone rogue, will be one of the most powerful things you do in life. It will be a process, so take your time, give yourself grace, and stay honest with God. Don't let your feelings run the show on this lesson. His word trumps what you feel and will be your guardian when your heart and spirit are being put back together after a season of rebellion.

Fifteen years ago, I remember telling the enemy, "You're going to regret the day you ever came for me." I challenge you to do the same. Let the enemy know he is going to pay for every lie he ever whispered in your ear to try to distract, delay, or deceive you.

As you walk this out, here is an anthem to shout along the way:

You've taken down so many others
Oh but you'll know my name when you see
And in these ashes I'm stronger still
You'll learn to fear my pain, yeah you will.
- Diamonds by Johnnyswim

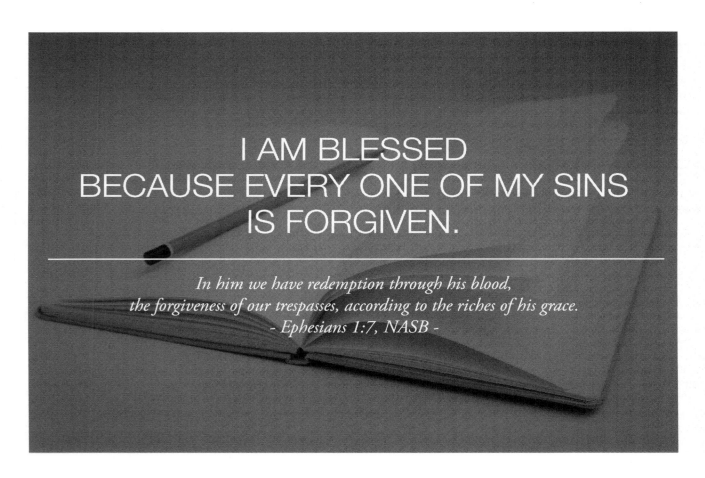

I AM BLESSED
BECAUSE EVERY ONE OF MY SINS
IS FORGIVEN.

In him we have redemption through his blood,
the forgiveness of our trespasses, according to the riches of his grace.
- Ephesians 1:7, NASB -

I HAVE BEEN FORGIVEN
AND SET FREE FROM
THE CYCLE OF SIN AND DEATH!

*When you were dead in your sins, you were not set free
from the sinful things of the world. But God forgave your sins
and gave you new life through Christ.*
- Colossians 2:13, NLV -

AS I BRING ALL MY SIN INTO THE LIGHT, HE IS FAITHFUL TO FORGIVE AND CLEANSE ME.

---

*If we confess our sins, he is faithful and just to forgive us our sins
and to cleanse us from all unrighteousness.*
- I John 1:9, NASB -

GOD CHOOSES NOT TO REMEMBER MY SIN. HE DOES NOT HOLD MY PAST AGAINST ME; IT'S NOT IN HIS NATURE.

I will not remember their sins and wrong-doings anymore.
- Hebrews 10:17, NLV -

I AM FORGIVEN AND GOD HAS DECLARED ME *NOT GUILTY!*

Finally, I confessed all my sins to you and stopped trying to hide my guilt. I said to myself,
"I will confess my rebellion to the LORD." And you forgave me! All my guilt is gone.
- Psalm 32:5, NLT -

I GENEROUSLY FORGIVE AND RELEASE OTHERS FROM THEIR SINS AGAINST ME. I DO NOT KEEP SCORE.

---

*I generously forgive and release others from their sins against me.
I do not keep score. Be kind to one another, tenderhearted,
forgiving one another, just as God in Christ also has forgiven you.*
Ephesians 4:32, NASB

*Then Peter came up and said to him, 'Lord, how often will my brother sin against me, and
I forgive him? As many as seven times?' Jesus said to him, 'I do not say to you seven times,
but seventy times seven.'*
Matthew 18:21-22, NASB

WITH GOD'S HELP, I EXTEND FORGIVENESS. I WILL NOT REPAY EVIL FOR EVIL.

... not returning evil for evil or insult for insult, but giving a blessing instead;
for you were called for the very purpose that you might inherit a blessing.
- I Peter 3:9, NASB -

I AM CALLED TO FORGIVE OTHERS AS GOD FORGAVE ME.

For if you forgive others their transgressions, your heavenly Father
will also forgive you. But if you do not forgive others,
then your Father will not forgive your transgressions.
- Matthew 6:14-15, NASB -

LIVING RECONCILED AND AT PEACE WITH OTHERS IS A HIGH PRIORITY TO GOD AND TO ME!

This is how I want you to conduct yourself in these matters. If you enter your place of worship and, about to make an offering, you suddenly remember a grudge a friend has against you, abandon your offering, leave immediately, go to this friend and make things right. Then and only then, come back and work things out with God.
- Matthew 5:23-24, MSG -

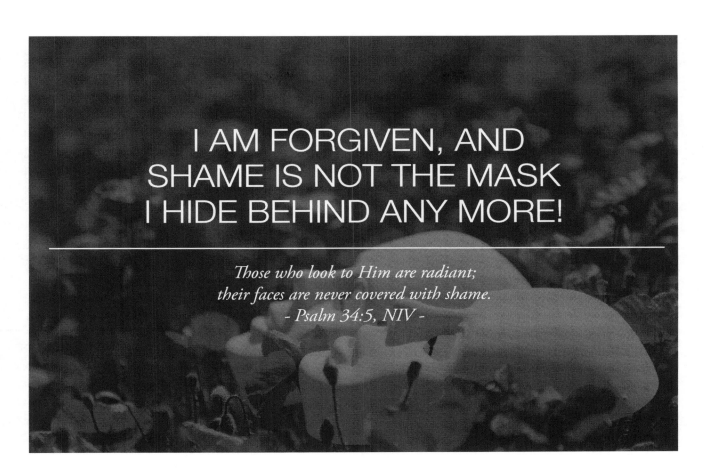

I AM FORGIVEN, AND
SHAME IS NOT THE MASK
I HIDE BEHIND ANY MORE!

Those who look to Him are radiant;
their faces are never covered with shame.
- Psalm 34:5, NIV -

TAKE A MOMENT
TO REFLECT

———————

Are you quick to forgive others? Are you quick to forgive yourself?

———————————

Do you believe God is quick to forgive you?
Is there an area of your life you feel like He can't fully forgive you?

———————————

Is perfection or progress your goal?

———————————

Is there any area of your life you want to see
God *fully* redeem and make new?

When perfectionism is driving, shame is always riding shotgun.

- Brené Brown -

REDEMPTION

Guilt, shame, and regret are three of the main weapons I see the enemy use to keep the body of Christ from moving forward in life. These three tactics can be slippery for several reasons.

First, they can masquerade as a righteous response after we sin. Yes, you read that right. Guilt and shame are not Godly responses to our sin. The Bible is very clear that when we sin, He is looking for conviction, a genuine, repentant heart, and asks us to go and sin no more. It is very simple! He does not hold sin over our heads to motivate us to "do better." He is really good at moving on and we need to learn to do the same.

Second, the enemy uses them "on cycle" against us. Meaning, he knows that guilt and shame pack a powerful punch so he will pull them out at strategic moments in our lives to shift our focus (off Christ and onto ourselves) and cloud our motivations. This is why it can feel like you are habitually sinning and not gaining victory in certain areas of your life. It's his "cycle approach." Don't believe this lie!

Third, sometimes people choose to hold on to their guilt and shame because they:

1) think it will keep them from sinning again
2) believe it is an indicator that they are, at least, trying to change
3) think it will keep them safe
4) believe they will never be free from their cycle of sin/repent
5) believe they need to pay penitence for their sin

False. Guilt and shame will never be good motivators or leaders in your life.

Finally, guilt and shame address and attack who you are (sons and daughters of God) versus what you have done (sin). This is why it is very important that when you sin you repent, receive your forgiveness, and *move on!* Guilt and shame do not get to name you. The Lord has already declared you fully forgiven and redeemed.

HE MAKES ALL THINGS NEW!

And He who sits on the throne said,
"Behold, I am making all things new."
He said, "Write, for these words are faithful and true."
- Revelation 21:5, NASB -

GOD HAS GIVEN ME A FRESH START, AND I'M TAKING HIM UP ON IT! NO MORE LOOKING BACK!

Now we look inside, and what we see is that anyone united with the Messiah gets a fresh start, is created new. The old life is gone; a new life burgeons!
- II Corinthians 5:16-17, MSG -

I WILL TELL MY TESTIMONY LOUD AND PROUD!

Let the redeemed of the LORD say so …
- Psalm 107:2a, NASB -

BECAUSE HE RESCUED ME, MANY WILL TRUST IN HIM!

He lifted me out of the pit of despair, out of the mud and the mire.
He set my feet on solid ground and steadied me as I walked along.
He has given me a new song to sing, a hymn of praise to our God. Many will see
what he has done and be amazed. They will put their trust in the Lord.
- Psalm 40:2-3, NLT -

HE HAS FORGIVEN AND CLEANSED ME! I AM PURE, LIKE FRESH FALLEN SNOW.

"Come now, let's settle this," says the LORD. "Though your sins are like scarlet, I will make them as white as snow. Though they are red like crimson, I will make them as white as wool."
- Isaiah 1:18, NLT -

GOD RESCUED ME!
NO MORE WANDERING ...
I HAVE FOUND MY HOME IN HIM.

God rescued us from dead-end alleys and dark dungeons. He's set us up in the kingdom of the Son he loves so much, the Son who got us out of the pit we were in, got rid of the sins we were doomed to keep repeating.
- Colossians 1:13-14, MSG -

MY STRENGTH COMES FROM THE LORD; I CAN DEPEND ON HIS STRENGTH!

He makes me strong again. He leads me in the way of living right with Himself which brings honor to His name.
- Psalm 23:3, NLV -

I AM REDEEMED, AND LED BY HIS LOVINGKINDNESS TODAY!

In your lovingkindness You have led the people whom You redeemed;
In Your strength You have guided them to Your holy habitation.
- Exodus 15:13, NASB -

NEW GRACE AND NEW MERCY AWAIT ME EVERY MORNING!

The faithful love of the Lord never ends! His mercies never cease.
Great is his faithfulness; his mercies begin afresh each morning.
- Lamentations 3:22-23, NLT -

NO MATTER MY PAST,
HE CLOTHES ME TODAY WITH
STRENGTH AND DIGNITY!

She is clothed with strength and dignity,
and she laughs without fear of the future.
- Proverbs 31:25, NLT -

TAKE A MOMENT
TO REFLECT
———

Is there any area of your life
that you are carrying guilt or shame?

———————————

How good are you at letting things go?

———————————

Does grace have a voice in your life?

———————————

Does receiving grace and giving grace come easy in your life?

To live is the rarest thing in the world. Most people exist, that is all.

- Oscar Wilde -

DREAMS + FUTURE

Have you ever stopped to think about the dreams that keep you up at night? The things in your life that ignite your passion and could keep you talking for hours?

For some, dreaming for more than what is in front of them is the challenge. They're occupied with the demands of the day, and they struggle to believe life could be any more than the daily grind of Monday through Friday. For others, dreaming about their future keeps them living there and they struggle to be present today. In short, they end up living in fantasyland and being useless to the world around them today.

Whichever category you might fall into, the bottom line is your dreams are intimately linked to God. What matters to you, matters to Him. No matter how big or small, God is up to speed on what makes your mind and heart spark. It is vital you know and believe *He is with you* in the dreaming and *He is leading you* in it.

How we carry our dreams is where the rubber will meet the road for many of us. You see, most of our days are filled with *normal* life: getting up, going to school or work, paying the bills, and washing the dishes. I call this adulting and how we do this matters to God. However, as we adult, it is important for us to remember what God's word says about our capacity, future, and life overall.

Leaning into God with your dreams is a delicate lean. It takes *courage* to believe beyond what you can see, it takes *perseverance* to try something new once you have failed, and it takes an ability to *wait* on God's grace, timing, and anointing to hit your life in due season. So, as you adult, call to remembrance what He has to say about your life. Keep your dreams in front of you, and do not let mold grow on them while you wait and adult! Steward them in such a way that when God hands you the baton, you'll look at Him and say, "I'm ready to run! Let's go!"

GOD KNOWS WHAT HE IS DOING WITH MY LIFE! MY FUTURE IS DRIPPING WITH HOPE!

For I know the plans I have for you," declares the Lord, "plans to prosper you and not to harm you, plans to give you hope and a future.
- Jeremiah 29:11, NIV -

ANYTHING IS POSSIBLE!

For nothing will be impossible with God.
- Luke 1:37, NASB -

WHAT GOD STARTS, HE FINISHES!

---

*For I am confident of this very thing, that He who began a good work
in you will perfect it until the day of Christ Jesus.*
- Philippians 1:6, NASB -

GOD WILL FULFILL HIS PURPOSE IN MY LIFE.
HE WILL NOT LEAVE ME ON MY OWN.

---

*The Lord will fulfill his purpose for me; your steadfast love, O Lord,
endures forever. Do not forsake the work of your hands.*
- Psalm 138:8, ESV -

GOD ESTABLISHES MY PATH.

The steps of a man are established by the LORD,
and He delights in his way.
- Psalm 37:23, NASB -

I AM NOT LATE OR EARLY, BUT RIGHT ON TIME IN LIFE.

He has made everything beautiful in its time.
- Ecclesiastes 3:11a, NIV -

MY LIFE IS MARKED BY PEACE.

You will go out in joy and be led forth in peace.
- Isaiah 55:12a, NIV -

AS I WALK WITH HIM, HE WITHHOLDS NO GOOD THING FROM ME! MY LIFE IS SMEARED WITH HIS GRACE AND GLORY!

For the LORD God is a sun and shield; The Lord gives grace and glory;
No good thing does He withhold from those who walk uprightly.
- Psalm 84:11, NASB -

I AM FULL OF COURAGE
BECAUSE GOD IS WITH ME.

Have I not commanded you? Be strong and courageous.
Do not be afraid; do not be discouraged, for the LORD your God
will be with you wherever you go.
- Joshua 1:9, NIV -

I WAS BORN
FOR GREAT ADVENTURE!

... but the people that know their God shall be strong, and do exploits.
- Daniel 11:32b, ASV -

TAKE A MOMENT
TO REFLECT

———

What are the dreams in your heart? What keeps you up at night?
What would you do if you weren't afraid?

———————————

How are you stewarding those dreams?
What can you do now to prepare?

———————————

Do you struggle to dream beyond what you can see?
Do you struggle with living in fantasyland?

———————————

If God were to hand you your dreams on a silver platter,
would you be ready today? Why or why not?

FINAL THOUGHTS

"I don't think the way you think. The way you work isn't the way I work." God's Decree. For as the sky soars high above earth, so the way I work surpasses the way you work, and the way I think is beyond the way you think. Just as rain and snow descend from the skies and don't go back until they've watered the earth, doing their work of making things grow and blossom, producing seed for farmers and food for the hungry, so will the words that come out of my mouth not come back empty-handed. They'll do the work I sent them to do, they'll complete the assignment I gave them.

- Isaiah 55:11, MSG -

I'm so glad you said yes to God and yes to His word! I pray these pages have been life to your bones and infused hope in your spirit.

My prayer for you: May you forever be anchored in truth. May you carry the kind of freedom that makes people stop in their tracks. May His words never return void in your story. May your life shout of His love and grace! May you introduce others to Him as freely as He introduced Himself to you. May walking with Him be your greatest adventure. May His goodness, mercy, and faithfulness always be in the rearview mirror of your life. Amen and *amen!*

For all the promises of God find their Yes in him. That is why it is through him
that we utter our Amen to God for his glory.
- I Corinthians 1:20, ESV -

ABOUT MORAL REVOLUTION

VISION

Our vision is to see a revolutionary shift in the way every individual understands, values and stewards purity and morality. This shift will help establish the safest, healthiest and purest generation that has ever walked the face of the earth. It is these individuals who embrace this divine wisdom that will break unhealthy mindsets, free mankind to value purity, honor marriage and empower wholeness in every family.

IMAGINE

We envision a society that celebrates true femininity and masculinity, lives from virtues and protects the pre-born. We dream of a world where there is no sexually transmitted disease, and where poverty and single-parent homes are a thing of the past. We imagine a planet where child abuse, pornography, prostitution and sex slavery are archaic, urban legends…a culture where every orphan is placed in a healthy home, and a world where righteous men and women lead every realm of society. This is the only kind of revolution that will restore the human race back to its God-given identity, dignity and purpose.

STAY CONNECTED WITH US

 Facebook.com/
MoralRevolution

 @MoralRevolution

 @MoralRevolution

 MoralRevolution.com

 Youtube.com/
MoralRevolutionInc

 Newsletter

ADDITIONAL

THE NAKED TRUTH ABOUT SEXUALITY

A practical, Biblical guide to understanding God's original design for sexuality. This shame-free, hope filled, entertaining and informative resource will answer key questions often pondered but never asked.

LET'S TALK ABOUT IT: SEXUALITY

A complete 6 week course designed to help you transform your community's view and understanding of healthy sexuality. It contains a 6-Session DVD set, Teacher Guide, and Student Guide.

RESOURCES

40 DAY JOURNEY TO PURITY

A 40-day guide to equip you to walk in a greater understanding of how God created you, and His design for sexuality, relationships, health and freedom in every area of your life.

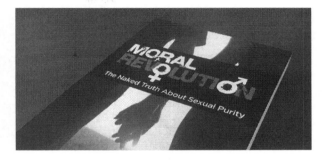

MORAL REVOLUTION

A honest and intimate overview training manual that will equip you to survive the battlefield of your own sex drive, overcome the power of peer pressure, and push back the cesspool of distorted cultural values.

Made in the USA
Lexington, KY
05 January 2018